EXPLORING THE GREAT LAKES

CONSERVING
THE GREAT LAKES

Gareth Stevens
PUBLISHING

By Walter LaPlante

Please visit our website, www.garethstevens.com. For a free color catalog of all our high-quality books, call toll free 1-800-542-2595 or fax 1-877-542-2596.

Library of Congress Cataloging-in-Publication Data

LaPlante, Walter.
Conserving the Great Lakes / by Walter LaPlante.
p. cm. — (Exploring the Great Lakes)
Includes index.
ISBN 978-1-4824-1207-9 (pbk.)
ISBN 978-1-4824-1190-4 (6-pack)
ISBN 978-1-4824-1431-8 (library binding)
1. Great Lakes (North America) — Juvenile literature. 2. Ecology — Great Lakes (North America) — Juvenile literature. I. Title.
F551.L37 2014
977—d23

First Edition

Published in 2015 by
Gareth Stevens Publishing
111 East 14th Street, Suite 349
New York, NY 10003

Copyright © 2015 Gareth Stevens Publishing

Designer: Michael J. Flynn
Editor: Kristen Rajczak

Photo credits: Cover, p. 1 The Asahi Shimbun Premium Archive/Getty Images; pp. 4, 5, 18, 24, 28 courtesy of NOAA; p. 6 http://en.wikipedia.org/wiki/File:Lithobates_pipiens.jpg; p. 7 http://en.wikipedia.org/wiki/File:Great_lakes_basin.jpg; p. 9 Grant Glendinning/ Shutterstock.com; p. 11 courtesy of the Library of Congress; p. 12 Phil Augustavo/E+/Getty Images; p. 13 Karen Gentry/Shutterstock.com; p. 15 Lester Balajadia/Shutterstock.com; p. 16 http://en.wikipedia.org/wiki/File:Peninsular_Dam_Ypsilanti.JPG; p. 17 Graham Taylor Photography/Shutterstock.com; p. 19 Benjamin Lowy/Getty Images; p. 20 http:// en.wikipedia.org/wiki/File:Dendroica_kirtlandii_-Michigan,_USA_-male-8_(5).jpg; p. 21 MikeLane45/Thinkstock.com; p. 23 Chris Walker/Chicago Tribune/McClatchy-Tribune/ Getty Images; p. 25 Michael Springer/Getty Images; p. 27 Dan Thornberg/Shutterstock.com; p. 29 mangostock/Shutterstock.com.

Printed in the United States of America

CPSIA compliance information: Batch #CS15GS: For further information contact Gareth Stevens, New York, New York at 1-800-542-2595.

CONTENTS

Words in the glossary appear in **bold** type
the first time they are used in the text.

TROUBLED WATERS

The health of Saginaw Bay on Lake Huron is a work in progress. A part of the Great Lakes, the bay is the largest **watershed** in Michigan, with about 240 miles (386 km) of shoreline. But pollution and other problems are upsetting the bay's **ecosystem**. Zebra and quagga mussels have overrun Saginaw's waters, in part causing harmful **algal blooms**. Muck made up of the algae collects on beautiful bay shorelines.

During the 1990s, a program to reduce pollution and protect nearby wetlands had some success. Cleanups of waterways around the bay continue today, though, proving how long lasting these problems can be.

quagga mussel

WHAT ARE THE GREAT LAKES?

The Great Lakes are the chain of lakes that extend from as far east as New York to as far west as Minnesota, and from Ontario, Canada, in the north, to Ohio and Indiana in the south. They include Lakes Huron, Ontario, Michigan, Erie, and Superior. Pennsylvania, Michigan, Wisconsin, and Illinois, as well as the St. Lawrence River in the Canadian province of Quebec, are also part of the Great Lakes watershed.

The problems in Saginaw Bay show how connected ecosystems are. The abundant algae grow because zebra and quagga mussels have filtered the water so well that sunlight reaches the bottom of the bay.

There's still much to be done in Saginaw Bay, but it's just one area in need of **conservation** in the huge Great Lakes region.

The Great Lakes are the largest surface of freshwater on Earth, covering about 94,250 square miles (244,106 sq km). Along their long shorelines are sand dunes, forests, and wetlands, which are all home to thousands of kinds of plants and animals. Even more **habitats** are part of the Great Lakes basin, which includes all the land and waterways that drain into the lakes. The many **tributaries** that empty into the lakes are home to reeds, fish, and amphibians, like the northern leopard frog.

northern
leopard frog

SAVE THE H2O!

Water is a nonrenewable resource. That means there's a limited amount of it. Nearly 40 million people depend on the Great Lakes for their drinking water. About 56 billion gallons (212 billion liters) of Great Lakes water are used for cities, farms, and industry, too. Taking care of this resource is very important.

This map shows how big the Great Lakes basin is. **Environmental** problems that occur anywhere in the watershed can easily affect the Great Lakes.

HABITAT LOSS

More than 35 million people live along the shores of the Great Lakes in both the United States and Canada. However, in order for cities like Chicago, Illinois, to be built, habitats had to be destroyed. About two-thirds of wetlands near the Great Lakes have been harmed since 1800. Wetlands naturally filter water and protect shorelines from **erosion**, so their loss damages the whole region.

Within the Great Lakes basin, there are about 3,500 species of plants and animals. When forests are cleared for farmland or new suburban neighborhoods, the animals living there must find new homes and sources of food—or die.

GROWING CITIES

The rapid growth of a city is called urban sprawl. The Great Lakes' cities of Chicago and Toronto, Ontario, are two of the most sprawling cities in North America. In addition to habitat destruction, sprawl commonly results in increased air pollution from more people driving cars. There's also more trash and **sewage** to get rid of.

mallards

The Great Lakes wetlands are home to many waterfowl, including mallards, wood ducks, and Canada geese. Groups such as Ducks Unlimited work to restore wetlands that have been harmed and protect other areas. This helps keep waterfowl populations healthy.

ALL ABOUT POLLUTION

Chicago's sewer system dumps untreated sewage into Lake Michigan when there's a very heavy rainstorm. Though this doesn't happen too often, environmentalists want it to stop altogether. Chicago has had sewage issues since the 1800s when the city built the Chicago Sanitary and Ship Canal. However, this kind of pollution doesn't just happen in Chicago. Sewage is a pollution problem throughout the Great Lakes basin.

Another major source of pollution is farm runoff. Chemicals are often used to help crops grow better and keep pests away. Soil, excess chemicals, and animal waste drain into waterways when it rains. Other pollutants include waste from factories and garbage dumps.

ALGAL BLOOMS

Farm runoff contains **nutrients**—mostly nitrogen and phosphorus—that build up in the water. Too much of these nutrients causes algae to grow quickly. It may create a "dead zone" in the water where no animals or plants can live because there's no oxygen. Some of these large algae growths can be toxic to people. Lake Erie, Saginaw Bay, and Maumee River in Ohio are all areas with high levels of harmful algae.

In 1885, the Chicago Sanitary and Ship Canal was built to change the direction of the Chicago River to keep the city's sewage out of Lake Michigan. However, the states around Chicago were unhappy, as it sent the dirty water toward the Mississippi River.

iron ore mine

Many mining operations use chemicals that pollute the water and soil around them, and wastewater ponds leak. Northeast Minnesota has been known for iron ore mines since the 1880s and open-pit taconite mines since the 1950s. They've left the waters near Lake Superior with high levels of mercury and other pollutants.

Cleaning up the Great Lakes will take time, as the lakes are large and water flows out of the lakes only a little at a time. Pollution stays in their water for a long time and can build up! It takes about 2.6 years for pollutants in Lake Erie to leave the lake. For Lake Superior, it's far longer—191 years!

WHAT'S THE IMPACT?

Before a new mine can be built, its environmental impact is considered. The Environmental Protection Agency (EPA) and other groups look at how a mine would affect animal populations in an area, for example. The government weighs this information with the economic impact the mine is likely to have. If the project is allowed to go ahead, companies are told about pollution limit laws. They aren't always followed, however.

Environmentalists in Minnesota argued in 2013 that the jobs a new copper-nickel mine would bring to the state weren't worth the damage the mine would cause to the water in the area.

WATER QUALITY AND QUANTITY

The waterways of the Great Lakes region are home to more than 200 kinds of fish. Their health shows the health of their ecosystem—and many species' populations have fallen as water quality worsened. Lake whitefish stopped migrating to Lake Michigan almost altogether during the 20th century because of this and other reasons.

Improving water quality in the Great Lakes has been of great importance for more than 40 years now. In 1972, the Clean Water Act put pollution regulations in place that cities and industries, such as the steel factories ringing the Great Lakes, had to follow. Water quality is slowly getting better. In fact, lake whitefish have returned to Lake Michigan!

IT'S GETTING WARMER

Scientists say temperatures in the Great Lakes basin are slowly rising by a few degrees. Warmer temperatures cause more water loss, lowering water levels. The water is warming up, too. There's less ice cover in colder months, and more storms are occurring in the area. The main reason for these changes is **climate change.**

Most people in Ontario, Canada, get their drinking water from the Great Lakes. The Clean Water Act doesn't apply to Canada. Its Environmental Protection Act is similar to the United States' 1972 law, though.

Dams are another man-made way the Great Lakes water is being managed. Dams have been shown to harm habitats and wildlife, however, and some have been removed to better these conditions.

Water diversion is one hot topic that worries environmentalists. Water diversion is the movement of Great Lakes water through man-made canals or pipelines outside of the watershed or to different parts of the basin. There isn't much of this going on right now, but proposals to divert water from the Great Lakes continue to be presented. Many have been rejected.

In the future, it may be harder to stop water diversion. As the US population grows, the need for drinking water will, too. Water diversions from the Great Lakes could answer this need, though the lakes' water quantity would be affected.

Niagara Falls hydroelectric power plant

POWER!

Niagara Falls is one of the seven natural wonders of the world. The falls are a natural border between New York and Canada. They're also the site of a hydroelectric power plant, fueled by water in the Great Lakes basin. Hydroelectric power stations are found on the St. Marys and the St. Lawrence Rivers, too. Great Lakes water is used for cooling at nuclear power plants around the region as well.

INVASIVE SPECIES

An invasive species is a nonnative plant or animal introduced to an area that begins growing uncontrollably. These species often cause problems as they grow because their presence upsets the ecosystem. Invasive species might harm the health of people living nearby, consume other organisms' food supply, or crowd out native species.

From cattails to the sea lamprey, the Great Lakes have had a number of invasive species overrun their shores and depths. One of the best known of these is the zebra mussel. In 1988, these mussels were accidentally brought into Lake St. Clair, which connects to Lake Erie by the Detroit River. Since then, zebra mussels have spread into all the lakes, rivers, and canals in the region.

zebra mussel

WORN AWAY

Invasive species may displace native plants and cause erosion of the Great Lakes shorelines. The native plants have roots that hold soil in place, but if they're gone, the water and wind more easily wear away the beaches and dunes. Erosion of the shoreline puts Great Lakes habitats, such as the coastal marshes and lake plain prairies, in danger, too.

Asian carp are an invasive species causing much concern because they reproduce very quickly. The National Wildlife Federation (NWF) and some Great Lakes states are presently trying to separate the Great Lakes and Mississippi River permanently to stop the carp from moving further into the watershed.

SPECIES IN DANGER

Animals and plants in danger of dying out are called endangered species. A species may become endangered because of habitat loss, the introduction of invasive species, or pollution—all problems facing the Great Lakes basin. Overhunting and overfishing cause populations to fall, too.

Kirtland's warbler is one endangered bird that lives in Michigan, Wisconsin, and Ontario. It only makes its nest in the jack pine forests of these Great Lakes areas, though it winters in the Bahamas. In 1976, a plan to increase Kirtland's warbler populations was put in place. It included planting more jack pine and protecting the forest habitats already growing.

Kirtland's warbler

EMPTY YOUR TANK!

The United States and Canada are working together to stop invasive species from harming the Great Lakes further. Many of these species come into the lakes from **ballast water**. Regulations are being put into place requiring ships to seal ballast tanks or empty them before entering the Great Lakes waterways. The US Coast Guard is presently working on applying these standards across the United States.

Laws limiting hunting and fishing often help endangered species repopulate. The gray wolf, though still considered endangered by some groups today, is just one animal of the Great Lakes region that has increased in population due to these laws.

There are so many conservation issues in the Great Lakes region, it can seem like an impossible task to tackle them all. Since the 1970s, a great effort has been made to reduce pollution, improve water quality, and protect habitats and the animals that live there.

Conservation in the Great Lakes began before that, though. The lakes were valuable for transportation and, of course, their water. Around 1900, the increase in pollution as cities grew was noticeable. In 1909, Canada and the United States signed the Boundary Waters Treaty, which created an international committee to oversee the water quality and water flow of the Great Lakes.

LEGALLY CLEAN

In 1972, the Clean Water Act passed. That same year, the United States and Canada established the Water Quality Agreement. The agreement called for an end to toxic pollution that could harm people and wildlife. It was updated in 1987 to set up a plan to help particularly damaged areas. In 2012, the agreement was updated again as the Great Lakes Water Quality Protocol of 2012.

Scientists continue to study the Great Lakes in order to understand the ecosystem better. Here, a group of scientists lower a buoy to test the waters of Lake Michigan near Milwaukee, Wisconsin.

In 2008, all eight Great Lakes states and the Canadian provinces of Ontario and Quebec enacted the Great Lakes–St. Lawrence River Basin Water Resources Compact. The agreement states one of its purposes is "to act together to protect, conserve, restore, improve, and effectively manage the waters and water dependent natural resources of the basin." Another part states that more scientific research will be done to learn the best ways to accomplish this goal.

The compact and other laws make it easier for governments to oversee conservation efforts. It's very important to make sure everyone is following the rules because the actions of one area could affect the whole watershed.

WORKING TOGETHER

The compact is just one example of the United States and Canada working together. The Great Lakes are a natural border between the United States and Canada. In the spirit of the nations' peaceful, 5,525-mile (8,892 km) border, they have collaborated for more than 100 years to make and enforce laws about water quality, management, and use in the Great Lakes.

KIDS NEED CLEAN WATER

US and Canadian citizens often make their opinions of environmental issues known through protests and public meetings.

Here are a few efforts that aim to save the Great Lakes basin:

▷ States have laws against overfishing and overhunting to protect wildlife. In New York State, there are daily limits for catching some kinds of fish. It's also illegal to catch endangered or almost-endangered fish species such as the gilt darter, round whitefish, or mud sunfish.

▷ The EPA, Great Lakes Fishery Commission, and other government groups built an electric barrier to keep Asian carp out of Lake Michigan. Though traces of the fish have been found beyond the barrier, so far there isn't any proof that any Asian carp live past that point.

TAKING CHARGE

The Great Lakes Restoration Initiative is using millions of dollars from the US government to help save the Great Lakes. This includes cleaning up toxic waste, restoring habitats like wetlands, and fighting invasive species. Each year, certain areas are chosen for concentrated efforts. For 2013 and 2014, Deer Lake and Manistique River in Michigan and Waukegan Harbor in Illinois were some of the "areas of concern."

Commercial fishing was once big business in the Great Lakes. Today, fishing for sport is very common—but it must be regulated to keep fish populations safe.

▷ In 2013, the government of Ontario passed the Great Lakes Protection Act. It aims to "protect and restore" the environmental health of the Great Lakes–St. Lawrence River basin and help the community become more involved in conservation efforts.

▷ Wetlands in Monroe, Michigan, had been drained for farming. In 2010, Ducks Unlimited and the Michigan Department of Natural Resources began restoring the coastal wetlands and lake plain prairie there so they could again filter farm runoff and become home to wildlife. The more than 60 acres (24 ha) of wetlands were successfully restored.

WHAT CAN YOU DO?

You can help the Great Lakes today! Speaking out in favor of conservation at your school can educate others about the problems facing the Great Lakes. If an environmentally risky issue comes up in your area, you can write a letter to your congressperson explaining your point of view, too. Additionally, you can keep your community clean, recycle, and do other environmentally friendly things!

Conservation efforts will continue for years to come in the Great Lakes region. While progress may seem slow, over time these projects will make a big difference.

GLOSSARY

algal bloom: a quick increase in a population of algae, which are plantlike living things that are mostly found in water

ballast water: the water kept in tanks on ships to help keep them stable and balanced

climate change: long-term change in Earth's climate, caused partly by human activities such as burning oil and natural gas

conservation: the care of the natural world

ecosystem: all the living things in an area

environmental: having to do with the natural world. A person who cares about the environment is an environmentalist.

erosion: the act of wearing away by wind or water

habitat: the natural place where an animal or plant lives

nutrient: something a living thing needs to grow and stay alive

sewage: waste matter from buildings that is carried away through sewers

tributary: a stream or river that flows into a larger body of water

watershed: an area of land whose water drains into a particular river or waterway

BOOKS

Burgan, Michael. *Not a Drop to Drink: Water for a Thirsty World.* Washington, DC: National Geographic, 2008.

Latta, Sara L. *Keep Out! Invasive Species.* North Mankato, MN: Capstone Press, 2014.

Mooney, Carla. *Explore Rivers and Ponds!* White River Junction, VT: Nomad Press, 2012.

WEBSITES

Environmental Education for Kids
www.miwaterstewardship.org/youthstewards
Michigan's website about how to make a difference in your community has great ideas about conserving water and getting your friends involved, too.

Save the Lakes: Kids – Great Lakes Watershed
www.greatlakeswatershed.org/save-the-lakes-kids.html
Find tons of links to information about Great Lakes conservation, games, and ways you can help save the lakes.

INDEX